GREEN GRAPES

Black

HANDS

(Poetry and Prose about the San Joaquin Valley and Beyond)

BY JACKIE JOICE

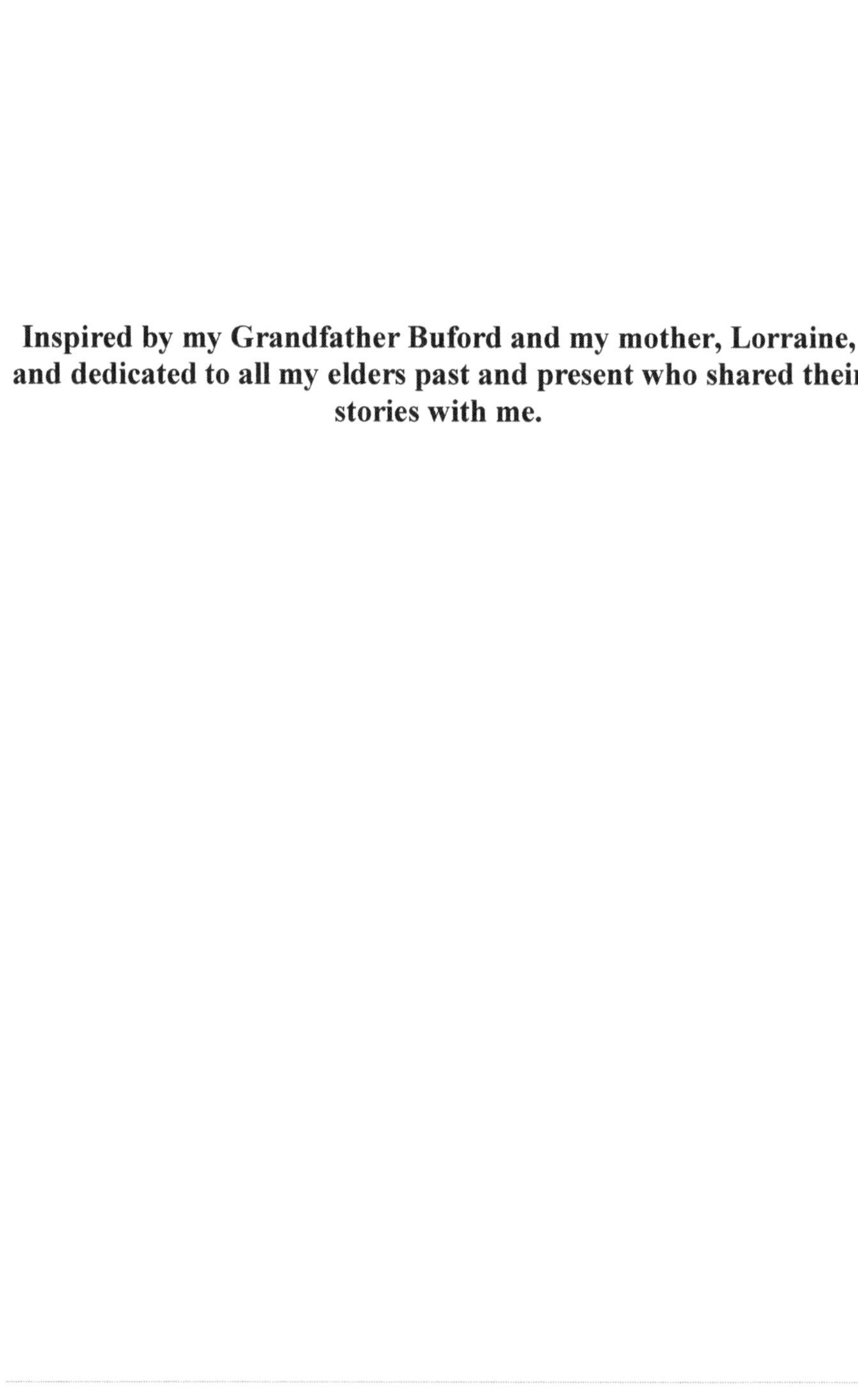

Inspired by my Grandfather Buford and my mother, Lorraine, and dedicated to all my elders past and present who shared their stories with me.

This book is also created with respect for the Tache Yokut people, the original occupiers of the region.

Glover Lane Press
Publishers Since January 2000
4570 Van Nuys Blvd Suite 573
Sherman Oaks, CA 91403
www.gloverlanepress.webs.com

Green Grapes Black Hands by Jackie Joice

ISBN-13: 978-0615817309
ISBN-10: 0615817300

Edited by Stefanie Spangler Buswell
Cover Design by Azaan Kamau
Photography Provided By Jackie Joice

The Mission of Glover Lane Press is to Uplift, Empower, Elevate the Masses and Provide American Jobs. Every book published by Glover Lane Press and its many imprints, is printed and manufactured in the United States of America, ensuring and maintaining American employment.

Acknowledgements

Thank you to Kevin Kennedy of the Hanford Sentinel Newspaper.

Thank you to my warrior poet and activist friend César A Cruz (teolol), for an amazing Foreword.

I would like to extend special thanks to my cousin Dra McDaniel for his endless encouragement and information regarding our family tree and our ancestors' journeys. I love you, man!

Thank you to cousin L.H. McDaniel for his moral support and optimism.

To my cousin Tim, for his extraordinary enthusiasm and optimism.

To my cousin Brent for attending my panel discussions and promoting my first book. That really meant a lot to me.

Thanks to my cousin Tracey Frazier and her daughter, Dominique Burrell, for purchasing, reading, and always promoting my work.

Inez Benegas for sharing a different side of my uncle William.

My aunt Judy for sharing our family history and for her warrior activism.

My uncle and writing partner in crime, Doc Fraz.

My cousin, Suzette for printing my first chapbook of poetry

My good friend and healer Gwenevere Bridge for her healing energy and generous donations and support.

My aunt Vickie Bradley for moral support and encouragement.

To Teresa Russ for shamelessly promoting my work and always stressing the importance of reading, as well as cultivating my interest in books since my early teens!

My friends Robyn McGee (author of the book *Hungry For More*), Noelle Green, Berit Jordahl, Lethia Cobbs, Terra Balthrop, Sylvia Beanes, Celina Curry, Larryssa Perry-Murdock, Tammy Munroe, Leo Buck, Romus Simpson, Tanya "Pinky" Pineda, Stacy

Jones, and Matais Pouncil for a wonderful Afterword, your sincere interest in my writing, your enthusiasm, and your friendship.

Also a huge thanks goes out to Tina Baldwin, Ronnie Kroell, Talibah Simmons, Cornflake B. Daze, Jaekoo Lee, Cat Mendez, Marla Deschenes, Katy Otto, Kanika Reynolds, Linda Watkins, Toni Ellis, Nicole Dukes, Earl Harville, Jennifer Leeper, Cat Mendez, Siue Moffat, and Sunshyne Raymaria.

To Ruth Thomasian (Executive Director and Founder of Project SAVE Armenian Archives. Inc.

A huge thanks to friends and family too many to mention here.

Thank you to the wonderful editor, Stefanie Spangler Buswell, for her patience and expertise.

Thank you to my husband for putting up with my crazy hours, yet giving me the space to create and to write.

For my mother for being my number-one publicist since birth.

And last, but not least, Azaan Kamau, CEO of Glover Lane Press, for believing in my work and assisting me with presenting it to the world.

Table of Contents

Introduction

The state of California has a rich and complex history that spans from the canneries in Northern California, across the farmlands in Central California, to the border of Mexico in Southern California. *Green Grapes, Black Hands* is loosely based on the center of California; the perceived "land of milk and honey" during the 1930s and early 1940s, when migration was fueled and extensive. Cities like Delano, Fresno, Hanford, Lemoore, Pixley, Selma, Tulare, and Visalia make up the vast Central California region, and some are a patchwork of farms and factories. Even today, most of the country's produce and dairy come from this region. Crops produced in this region consisted of grapes, garlic, almonds, onions, peaches, nectarines, plums, and cotton, just to name a few. In fact, the city of Selma is considered the raisin capitol of the world. These fruit crops in the San Joaquin Valley and the economic hardships in other states, like the Dust Bowl of Oklahoma and the Great Depression, drove the influx of migrant farm workers to Central California during this time.

Migrant laborers and farm worker are often associated only with Mexican and Filipino people. However, unearthed rich heritage of the Black experience and their labor contributions to Central California exists beneath the surface of the history books. This legacy is often focused solely on the labor in the cotton fields, especially in Corcoran, California.

According to the authors Mark Arax and Rick Wartzman of *The King of California*, "Between 30,000 and 40,000 black Okies arrived in the valley in the year after World War II, 7,000 of them settling in the Tulare Lake basin. Their migration west happened to come at the same time the federal government was implementing the Bracero program, allowing farmers to import seasonal guest workers from Mexico. From 1944 to 1954, the number of Mexicans toiling in the fields of California jumped from 36,000 to 84,000. Because there were enough crops in the San Joaquin Valley to sustain seven or eight months of work, the black Okies, like the Mexicans, hopped from harvest to harvest with a 150-mile radius. They thinned out the rows of cotton in May, dug up the onions and potatoes in June, picked grapes in July and August, and returned to the cottons fields in October." (page 264)

In any event, that these significant stories were lost in translation or just simply overlooked is bewildering. For example, my ninety-three-year-old grandfather, who was a tenant farmer and sharecropper born in Teneha, Texas, purchased his first vehicle, a 1935 Ford, for $325 after picking grapes for just a few months in Selma. During his time, laborers earned six cents per tray. He picked an average of two hundred trays a day in the sizzling-hot sun.

According to my grandfather, the farmers in Texas fed him dinner, but he had to sit on the back porch while he ate because he wasn't allowed in the house or through the front entrance because he was Black, and Jim Crow Laws forbid it. My grandfather stressed that even though the Texans fed him, the California farmers didn't provide dinner. Laborers had to bring their own food and store it among the grapevines. Before they arrived in Selma, my grandfather and his family lived in one of those infamous tent cities depicted in John Steinbeck's novel *The Grapes of Wrath*.

As a writer, journalist, and descendant of migrant workers, tenant farmers, and trailblazers, I have a responsibility and moral obligation to give a voice to the unheard. It is my duty to document and share a historical past that's been hidden and overlooked for decades in Central California. These Black laborers worked hard to earn a living and support their large families during harsh economic times, not to mention they did so in the face of unforgiving racism.

There's no doubt that *Green Grapes/Black Hands* will challenge the current stronghold on past written accounts of migrant workers and pioneers in Central California. But at the same time, the book will hopefully shed light on the rich history of immigrants—Armenian, Indians, Italians, and Japanese, to name a few—and migrant workers who have contributed to the building of Central California's economic and cultural foundation. Many of the descendants of these families still reside in these areas, and some of these trailblazers are still living. If these younger generations of Black pioneers and trailblazers knew what their grandparents, great-grandparents and great-great-grandparents endured, perhaps they would be instilled with a new sense of pride. For decades, a large patch of fabric has been missing from the annals of history regarding Black migrants, laborers, and pioneers in the Central California quilt, and I would like to sew it in.

Foreword

I begin with italics to accentuate Jackie's words. These are Jackie Joice's own words spliced together in this foreword to tell an *un*told story of Black farmers, sharecroppers, families, and people at the center of California. It is her story—her parents', grandparents', and great-grandparents' story. It honors Black history in the U.S. without the typical discussion of slavery and white agency at the hands of Black submission. There are people on their knees in this book, praying and cultivating the land and their story.

In "*Green Grapes/Black Hands,*" Jackie *sows*
an *unearthed rich history*
through her *feminine psychic self.*
She quilts the *Black experience*
filled with *sweat and bone*
from the Central Valley to Los Angeles,
where faith had her
collecting aluminum cans for Jesus.

Jackie speaks of a place
where *dandelion wishes*
combat a *Mother Earth*
in desperate need of a *papsmear,*

a place where womyn
can't take *short cuts* in allies
for fear of what lurks in the unknown,

a place where *crystal*
met(h) the hood
and *Death tailgated*
a close friend to his grave.

In this place,
Backwoods'- remedies

bring healing,
whether from cow's dung
or whiskey in the milk.

In this book,
callous hands turn the page
on ol' Jim Crow narratives
to find a people
toiling the earth for themselves
with pride, nostalgia, and memory
so that seven generations from now,
their offspring
will no longer be the afterthought
of California's rich Black history.
They are front and center,
Presente,
adding more than just a grain of salt
to the earth,
and it is that contribution
that Jackie Joice honors.
And it merits study,
reading, and
embracing
to enrich all of our understandings
of who came before us,
who is *still* here,
and who will be the caretakers of this land
whose name did not begin with America or the US.

This is the history of Turtle Island
of Anahuac
of Aztlán
of the Diaspora of Africa.

This is the history of those who plant seeds
and matter.

This is our history,

and it is about time
we learn it.

. . .

César A. Cruz (teolol)
Co-Founder, Homies Empowerment
Educational Leadership Doctoral Candidate, Harvard University

Pomegranate Sunrise

It was early in the morning,
shortly after sunrise.
I sped down Highway 41 with pomegranate fields to my right.
The auspicious fruit reflected red slivers of sunlight.
Driving in thirty-something-degree weather, with my window down.
Few cars on the road, and my speakers' bumpin' sounds.
Coffee was brewing in many kitchens at that time.
Yet once the fog lifted,
the Chi of Kings County shifted

Kings River Blues (Part One)

This poem isn't about sunsets and sunrise
or landscapes and otherwise.
It's about the blood of grapes and hard
labor, sweat, and bone in scorching fields,
accompanied by cheap wages for picking
pounds and pounds of cotton and grapes.
Wine grapes that were processed with
mechanical feet,
smashed.
It's about blood-speckled white afro puffs
being picked for Rodeo Drive clothing
stores.
It's about white afro puffs being picked to
the hymns of harmonicas bought in Texas
for twenty-five cents.
It's about whore rates for seamstresses
working twelve hours straight,
blood from Dust Bowl survivors.
Migrating
herd
hooves
sheep
like cattle packed in tents with grit.
It's solely about the perspective of a

dislocated
city chick to country parents,
but not country like down in the Mississippi
Delta country,
but Central California country.
This poem is no click of your boots to the
Midwest type of Oz.
This poem is about the heartland of
California,
about bodies in fields, picking green grapes
with black hands.
I siphon whiskey from these grapes,
and now I am drunk with
the Kings River Blues.

One-Two Punch

I got that fighter blood,
like my grandfather,
who used to be a boxer
and a chef while he lived in Hanford.
He boxed in barns,
surrounded by hands holding
up cash,
betting,
sweating
shouting,
cheering.
My skills are like a Mustang,
wild and untamed.
I write Armageddon
when my worlds collide.
I put pen to paper,
dodging verbal bullets and knives.
I'm a dictionary assassin,
armed with words.
My tongue drops nouns and verbs
onto paper like fire bombs.
I'm slicing and dicing sentences
and baptizing the mic
with literary sermons.

I'm writing like my great uncle,
slanging poetry to the community,
Delivering a one-two punch
to the third eye and the senses.

Bee Venom

(based on one of my grandfather's nicknames, "Bumblebee")

Every time my grandfather coughed,
it sounded like he hacked out a
little piece of his soul.
His back is angled from aging bones,
while he sits and shares memories of a Texas-California journey.
His farm worker hands
picked grapes, cut vines,
and serenaded tribal ancestors.
He still whips out his harmonica,
even though his lungs are weak.
He still manages to blow
Southern notes
to the Kings River Blues,
the audition
for the soundtrack of his life.

(2013)

La Cañada de las Uvas

(The Grapevine)

Wild grapes grew along
the winding roads
once tread by hooves,
leather moccasins,
and hide boots.
Now there's a constant
flow of fumes and metal,
rubber to paved cement,
double yellow lines,
scuff and burn marks
acquired by
deaths by liquor or text.
There's no graffiti
on road signs
because it's
too desolate and parchment dry
with wild animals and darkness.
Too parchment dry with
creepy Hollywood-movie rest stops
and lack of lighting
that deter defacement.
I can't even count how many times
I've been through the Grapevine,

bundled up during winter,
blanketed while driving or riding
because of the temperature
dropping wild,
like California antelope.
I crave wild grapes and natural fruit now,
juice popping on my tongue,
tasty pulp.
I crave fruit, not cloned fruit absent of
fertile seeds that we should be spitting
back to Mother Earth.

(2013)

Mother Earth Needs a Pap Smear

I looked into the brown-colored sky and
thought about the blue we use to have.
Mother Earth needs a physical, a pap smear.
She's suffering from bad acne; her hair is falling out.
She has a hole in her head.
She's suffering, sinking, suffocating.
She's doing crack.
She's on Sunset Boulevard, pimpin' me and you.
Her chapped, cracked, and peeling lips cannot form the words for help
Her parchment-dry, rusty throat cannot swallow.
Death becomes her weary, worn out, rotund figure.
Food pollution, water pollution, air pollution, human pollution are overwhelming conditions
So you'd better fill out one or two of those petitions
For the revision of the earth.
Or else you can take your
recycled, re-used, re-defined, re-whatever
greetings cards and grocery bags
and throw them away,
because Mother Earth needs a pap smear.

(1993)

No Detours

(for Robin)

The zealots will probably condemn me to hell,
scrap my holey jeans,
and shove sacred water down my throat
But I can't help it,
because I enjoy how ocean water reflects
a full moon and how the waves
are rhythmic and slushy.
I enjoy the smell of pine, musty soil on starry nights,
and the incessant sound of crickets and occasional
grunts from bears.
The zealots will probably condemn me to hell
and burn me at the stake in the middle of an intersection.
Ignite the ingested holy water, and then I'll become
a Negro Molotov cocktail,
burning with desire.

No Shortcuts

(for Norma Lopez)

Whether if we're walking, running, or
hiding to avoid a familiar face,
we as women cannot duck into alleys
to observe the narrowness of walkways
or the beauty of flower pots that grace
balconies, steps, and windowpanes.
Alleys aren't conducive to women,
Because at the blink of an eye,
the strike of a match,
or the click of a streetlight,
we can become history
between the pages of local newspapers.
And the rings of our cell phones
go unanswered.
Then they're checked for the last call dialed.
We don't have the luxuries of
shortcuts or saving time.
That wasn't in our contract,
Because at the blink of an eye,
the strike of a match,
or the click of a streetlight,
our loved ones will look at
their watches and say, "She

was supposed to be here."
And they will never guess the
Unthinkable,
because we don't have the luxuries of
shortcuts or saving time.
That wasn't in our contract.
So maybe in another lifetime,
we can stroll through alleys during
sunny afternoons without constantly
looking over our shoulders
or tensing our muscles at the sound
of a stray dog rummaging through trash cans.
So maybe in another lifetime,
we won't have to walk swiftly
through alleys on sunny afternoons,
but stroll with ease and take shortcuts if we want to.

(2010)

She

I heard her when she left my womb.
It was a child's giggle that
jarred me out of my sleep at three a.m.
It was similar to the surround sound
of a stereo.
The laughter echoed like a church bell
during the hour of death.
The laughter faded,
and then she traveled back
into the universal womb,
and I, with my sacred feminine psychic self
fell back into denial,
closed my eyes,
and went back to sleep.

2007

Hair

Jackie, why did you cut your hair?
I liked it the "other way."
Jackie, are you going through something?
Jackie, are you ill?
Jackie, do you belong to a religious cult?
Jackie, are you a lesbian?
Jackie, why did you cut your hair?
I cut my hair
because I was tired of
frying
burning
cooking
crimping,
chopping,
cutting,
curling
pulling
stretching
gelling
slicking
pinning
relaxing
perming
and spending.
That's why I cut my hair.

What would Dionysus Think?

What would Dionysus
think if he knew that
grapes were growing, weaving, spreading
in chain-link
fences that connected South Los Angeles
backyards?
These were no table grapes being harvested
south of Hollywood, away from glamour and glitz,
but near lawn chairs and barbecue pits.
These were industry grapes
being plucked by copper fingers,
collected in beach pails and plastic bins,
not paper trays.
I remember eating purplish grapes,
carefully squeezing the green pulp
out their skin
onto my tongue.
I remember drops of juice carefully
muted by the swift
inertia of helicopter blades,
police sirens,
barking dogs,
and jive talking.
I remember a yellow kitchen with a deep

sink filled with grapes
being rinsed and prepared
for consumption and production
of an urban moonshine.
What would Dionysus think if he knew that
a slice of the San Joaquin Valley
was being produced and sipped by the lips
of a Black Okie named Two Mama and the
lips of Two Mama's friends and family?

Urban Redemption

I used to think that the end of the world
would happen during the middle of the night
as bony stray dogs
rummaged through trash and petty thieves
hustled hot merchandise.
I used to think that the end of the world
would happen during the middle of the night
after the last bag of popcorn popped
and televisions turned off
when suddenly
the black night peels back
and voluptuous, raw stars are exposed.
        Trumpet sounds thundering,
        frantic birds scattering,
        my small chest vibrating,
as I shout to my brothers in the next room,
"This is it! This is it!"
The ghetto awakens, and
        quick meteorite flashes
        light up my backyard.
I rise on my knees to peek out my bedroom window,
and I see Him,
standing huge and towering.
Will I kiss His punctured feet to

receive salvation?
Will I find fire and brimstone as the horned
underworld beast comes
bursting through
cracked sidewalks
and cluttered alleys
          with gaping jaws
          scooping up
          meth addicts, thieves, and whores?
Structures are crumbling,
trees are exploding,
and sewer pipes are spewing
baptismal water in the air.
My neighborhood is cleansed
in this urban redemption.

Summer Vacation Bible School

During childhood summers in South Central L.A.
I attended vacation bible school at the
church propped up at the end of my street.
Inside, the church was hot, like Jonah in the
belly of a whale.
I was quizzed on bible verses
and commandments.
I sang my heart out with the neighborhood kids.
"Yes, Jesus loves me!"
At least that's what they told me
while I ate free lunch
and played softball in
the vacant dirt lot next door.
We worked in the church's hot, cramped garage
on wooden tables,
cutting and clipping,
painting and pasting
pasta and beads on crafts for Jesus.
These religious ornaments
adorned with buttons, shells,
and macaroni were indicative of our spiritual zeal.
We worked feverishly, chafing our fingertips and biting the corners of our lips while
concentrating, sweating, and gluing together
these crafts for Jesus.
Yes, Mrs. Dudley made us believe that our

diligent efforts on our crafts would bring us
closer to Him.
So, I still have crafts
packed away in dusty storage boxes,
just for back-up,
just for security.

Aluminum Cans

On the last Friday of every month,
our principal, Sister Patricia,
decided that we could wear our own
clothes on one condition:
if students brought fifty or more aluminum
cans to school for recycling.
So on the last Friday of every month,
uniform free,
I'd wait at the bus stop with a large
black trash bag.
When the bus arrived, I hauled the thick
black trash bag of clanging cans that
I'd collected from home and neighbors to the nearest available seat.
Sometimes, I would hear the clanging of cans
coming from the back of the bus,
which indicated that other schoolmates
were aboard.
I would rush to the back,
squeezing between passengers, and join my
comrades in this aluminum-can revolution.
On the last Friday of every month,
my blue plaid skirt and thrift-store-looking
sweater remained at home, wrinkled and dirty.
On the last Friday of every month,

among briefcases, folded strollers, and perverts,
there we were, rows of trash-bag-holding junior high school students
with tight jeans, halter tops, sneakers, and
crucifixes on the bus, with aluminum cans
for Jesus.

Dandelions

I believed dandelions made wishes come true,
even for me,
even for my neighborhood.
I searched alone because no one believed
in my front-yard fantasies
among the street sounds
of barking dogs
and arguing neighbors.
I pulled them up,
closed my eyes tight,
and blew,
and blew.
And the dandelion seeds
traveled on the air
on ghetto notes
and floated between
rented houses,
hanging clothes,
peeling billboards, and buildings.
And I blew and blew.
No, these dandelion seeds
never touched the ground.
They stuck to the wings of sparrows
and floated into space among the stars,

because I blew and I believed.

I blew, and I believed

I knew my wishes would come true.

Because I was taught to dream.

The Violet Fire

I'm still standing,
Even though there's a crack in the terrordome.
I'm still standing, arms outstretched,
eyes closed, stigmata style,
amidst the skyscraper erections
and wireless connections.
But that electro-BS don't matter.
Flick the chatter,
because once I bowed down
on bent knees and lowered my head
among the walking dead—
in the chaos of starched business suits,
texting, Skyping, cell phones, and
matrix stew—
I dipped the tip of my tongue into the Nile
River and sensed the power of the Holy Spirit.
The *espiritu santo*
The *ruach hokodesh*
The *soom soom crum crum*
Suddenly, the clocks and streetlights stopped,
because the crowds wanted to touch me,
feel the lightning in my blood,
see the sun in my eyes,
the sway in my thighs.

St. Germain, I'm calling, falling, floating,
and causing brake lights and canceled flights.
Forked tongue and trickery
can't dowse the flames of the violet fire, ya see?
So stop complainin'
and embrace the power of the feminine,
the vaccine for mindless conditioning.
You'll start skankin' through metallic plumes of smoke,
military tanks, and hurricane notes that are
still flooding our psyche, ya follow me?
Reach within,
clean your slate,
commit random acts of kindness,
and like Ani DiFranco sang, "Anticipate."
I'm still standing, even though there's a crack in the terrordome.
Suddenly, the suits, and clocks, and streetlights stopped,
because now I'm free.

(2008)

Hogs

Anytime I see hogs,
Sus scrofa domestica
they evoke memories
of my grandfather throwing them scraps of
hospital leftovers.
Hogs evoked memories of quality
slop dumped in wooden feeding bins.
My grandfather was a chef
at the local hospital
for decades.
We rode in his pickup truck
belt buckled and cramped.
He and my brother wore
white singlets and blue jeans
and fed dozens of hogs.
sus scrofa domestica
They fed hogs when the
sun barely peeked over
Hanford's horizon,
but still warm
in the early morning.
sus scrofa domestica
I can still remember the smell
of the hogs,
the feed,
the slop.

I can still remember the sounds
of their mealtime,
the grunts, the squeals.
I can still remember
everything.
sus scrofa domestica

Sunshine's First Road Trip and the Smell of Cow Manure

January 2010

"Ahhhhhhhhh, there's nothing like the pungent smell of cow manure so early in the morning," I texted to my friends as I sat in the backseat with my three-month-old daughter, Sunshine. Of course, she was fast asleep. Car seat plus movement equals sleep, even without the Bob Marley music my husband played as we headed North on the Five. Car seats induce sleep better than any dropper of chamomile tea. I wish I had a car seat for myself! I had my watercolor pencils, my animal medicine book, three journals, and a traveling cup of fenugreek tea and, of course, my cell phone to keep my friends updated on my first trip to the San Joaquin Valley with Sunshine.

Unfortunately, the smell of cow manure is nostalgic for me. It reminds me of the times when my mom, brothers, and I headed to Hanford, California, to visit my grandfather, cousins, and aunts. Hanford is located in Central California and is a little under two hundred miles north of Los Angeles. Hanford is a patchwork of almond orchards, grape and corn fields, dairies, and pig farms. It's a small town that still has dangling traffic signals in some areas.

My mother and grandmother were born there. My maternal great-grandfather settled in Hanford sometime in the early 1900s after leaving Atlanta, Georgia.

Sunshine is my first child, and I wanted her to visit Hanford. Besides, according to her astrological chart, she supposed to enjoy traveling. We headed to Fresno first so that Sunshine could meet her great-grandfather. My grandfather turned ninety this year. My husband and I packed the night before our first journey with Ms. Sunshine. In fact, she had her own luggage. We were planning to stay with my cousin Shari, in Hanford. So I packed some warm long johns and a papoose for Sunshine because it can get as cold as the arctic in my cousin Shari's house. Not only that, it was still winter. Although we were staying for only one night, I packed extra clothes for Sunshine, in case an asteroid suddenly impacted the 5 Freeway. A can of formula, in case of a sudden global-warming blizzard. Twelve diapers, in case there was a major earthquake and sections of California collapsed into the Pacific Ocean. Well, you get the point. I made sure I had an excess of everything. Saturday morning, we ran a little late, and I prayed that Sunshine wouldn't poop until we reached our destination. Well, she pooped right on time, because we just had exited the Grapevine. So my husband changed her diaper in the front seat of the car in the parking lot of a Jack in the Box restaurant.

We finally reached my grandfather's house. It was like a museum to Sunshine. My grandfather had been in that house for years. I had to nurse Sunshine, so I went into my grandfather's bedroom, and Sunshine couldn't even focus on my breasts! She just had too much stuff to look at. Anyhow, I took some pictures of Sunshine with her great-grandfather, and my grandfather's wife prepared lunch for us. My husband and I enjoyed fried catfish, string beans, potato salad, and grape punch! Before we headed to Shari's house, we stopped in Selma, the raisin capitol of the United States. My great-aunt Louise lives in Selma, and she hadn't met Sunshine, either. Selma is just a little south of Fresno, but north of Hanford. My great-aunt Louise was happy to meet Sunshine. She even offered a home remedy for Sunshine's gas—a couple of drops of whiskey in her milk!

On our way back home, we stopped in Lebec for a snack, and I gave Sunshine a breast milk appetizer in the backseat. Breast milk must have kryptonite or something in it, because it knocks her out as if she'd just smoked a big fat joint! Needless to say, she slept the entire ride home, and I even got in a couple of zzz's.

Root Woman

(for my daughter)

I may be asked if I have found God
since this little ray of sunshine
made her way through the cosmos
and implanted herself in my womb.

She now props her foot on my shoulder
as she sucks milk from my breasts
and plays while she drinks.

I may be asked if I have found God
since she smiles at me on early mornings,
when my tongue is overnight dry and my vision blurred.

I answer, “God never left.”

(2010)

A Bundle of Sunshine

Once we exited Grapevine Road
and parked in the lot of a
Jack in the Box,
I breastfed my daughter in the backseat
of the car
during the last months of winter
in the city of Lebec.
We were on our way to introduce
Sunshine to her great-grandfather,
the grandfather
who once traveled to Oregon,
just to pick strawberries,
just to work,
just to feed his children.
He anticipated my visit
with the new addition to the family,
another descendant
new
ripe
like freshly picked fruit birthed into his lineage.

(2013)

Broke Down in Lebec

(For Winston)

I missed those days when
you would come over and bathe
a spring mix of greens in vinegar.
You would be dancing to music
while dicing, chopping,
and grating preparations
for dinner.
We cooked as friends,
conversing over red wine and whiskey.
Then, one month, there you were,
with black trash bags and
suitcases filled with
your life stuffed in your Beemer.
During your last visit before you headed to
Northern Cal,
you still had the optimism of a dreamer.
We bid you farewell,
and then you sped off
Crystal Meth leaked
from your radiator.
You sped down the 5 Freeway,
headed for a new future,
but I knew in my heart

you weren't clean.
Your guardian angels hopped on
celestial motorcycles
and followed you, clocking in overtime.
I wished you luck on your new life
because you were to work
in a California State prison,
administering medication,
when medication is what you needed,
when intervention is what you needed,
when deliverance is what you needed.
So your car broke down in Lebec.
Perhaps it was Creator giving you time
to reflect.
I will never know what your thoughts were
while you twiddled your fingers
in the cold,
alone,
thinking.
You were broke down in Lebec,
given time to reflect,
giving your angels a break,
but Crystal Meth was your fate.

When Winston Meth Crystal

2009

Crystal is Aphrodite, Lilith, Oshun, Erzulie, and Bastet, cloaked in a hooded black robe. She promises sweet sex and eternal orgasms. Crystal has many suitors, male and female.

Crystal can be found between the mattresses of seedy motels, on street corners, in the glove compartment, or in a teen's backpack. She offers several sleepless nights, indiscriminate sex, and the daily threat of death disguised as euphoria.

Over pancakes and coffee at a local café in Long Beach called The Potholder in late 2006 or early 2007, we had a conversation about crystal. This was not an unusual engagement, since Winston and I often indulged in coffee over deep conversations regarding politics, sex, and religion.

The revelation slipped in between the clatter of utensils and bells ringing from the door of the café. "Jackie, I need to tell you something," Winston stated.

I dabbed a piece of pancake in butter and syrup.

Winston took a long sip of coffee. He maneuvered and shifted in his seat as if we sat in a dimly lit bar with cigarettes hanging off our lips.

"I've been experimenting," Winston confessed.

"Experimenting with what?" I took a sip of my coffee.

"Experimenting with drugs," he answered.

"Okay, go ahead."

Winston proceeded to give me details of drug-laced stories involving porn actors and third parties. I didn't blink as he disclosed the sordid details of the double life he'd been leading.

"So what do you think?"

"Well…" I paused as I dabbed another slice of pancake in buttery syrup. "You are an adult, and you must be prepared for the consequences of your choices."

Winston had a history of inflating and creating elaborate stories about himself. He often said and did things just for shock value.

"That's it?" said Winston. "Aren't you shocked?"

"Well, what do you want me to say… or do? You want me to scold you or cuss you out? You're gonna do what you want to anyway"—I paused—"just be prepared for the consequences of your choices, especially since you know that you have a family."

When I think back on this conversation we had over pancakes and coffee, maybe I should have cussed Winston out. Maybe I should have displayed utter disgust when he told me about crystal, because maybe, just maybe, he would be here today if I had.

When Winston revealed that he was experimenting with the drug crystal meth, that's what I took it as—an "experiment." I had no idea how deeply in love Winston was with crystal. I had no idea of the depth of this love affair, until almost a year later, when Winston's brother called my husband and asked my husband to talk to Winston because he was out of control. My husband and I drove to a

Starbucks in the Inland Empire and met with Winston and his brother, Don. The meeting was short of a scene from The Jerry Springer Show or Maury Povich. We yelled over lattes and crumb cake. At one time, I stood and pointed at Winston with anger and disappointment.

Winston was always welcomed at our apartment, any time. If we were asleep, we just didn't answer the phone. The times he came over, who knows whether Winston was high or not. I could tell when someone was drunk or high from marijuana, but when it came to the more serious drugs, I had no idea. Later, other friends informed me about the signs and symptoms of crystal meth. One of those signs was an extreme craving for sugary foods, which explained why Winston devoured the Starbucks crumb cake the day of our disastrous meeting. I thought perhaps he was very hungry. However, I was wrong. It was a side effect of crystal meth. This is why so many meth users have deteriorating teeth.

In January of 2009, Winston dropped by early one morning. He sat on the brick steps of my house with a newspaper and smoked a cigarette, until I woke to open the door. When I let Winston in, I noticed his sullen face. He had lost a significant amount of weight, and his clothes were stained and worn. Winston was a great cook, so I asked him to cook us breakfast. Winston visited and cooked for me often in exchange for a typed letter, revised resume, or essay for a class. I put on a jazz radio station for Winston and brewed a pot of coffee, then waited for breakfast. Winston hummed to the music as he meticulously chopped potatoes and sautéed onions and mushrooms. He whizzed in the kitchen rhythmically from cabinet to refrigerator to cupboard, retrieving spices, eggs, and cooking utensils. He set the table with two matching plates and silverware. Once breakfast was ready, Winston and I sat and sipped our coffee.

"Jackie, I'm tired. I want to stop." Winston had constantly refused to go to rehab. He thought the rehabilitation process was a waste of time. Winston had worked as a mental health worker for thirteen years and possessed some knowledge of the system and drug abuse.

"Winston, you're working your guardian angel overtime. One day they're gonna throw in the towel," I replied.

Winston laughed, "Is this how you wanna go out? Is this how you wanna be remembered? Think about your daughter." We briefly sat in silence, and then I said, "I see a dark cloud over you."

He shunned my concerns and answered his cell as he walked out. After this visit, we didn't see Winston for days, and then one very windy and cold night in February, he showed up on our doorstep. He coughed and hacked incessantly. By then, I knew he was having withdrawals. My husband thought he had a cold. But from my previous conversations with Winston, I knew he hadn't stopped using, contrary to what he'd told my husband. Winston fell asleep on our couch and could not be removed. His body went into torpor. We left him there to sleep overnight, and he coughed and coughed, but never opened his eyes.

Winston slept for a day and a half. I took pictures of him as he lay on our couch as if he were in a coffin. When he finally woke, he was like a new person. He showered and sang loudly and happily in our shower. Then Winston left and headed to the unknown. Between Winston's unannounced visits, my brother was on leave from the military and stayed with us for a couple of weeks. My brother had met Winston on a few occasions, but didn't know him as well as my husband and I did. Brian convinced Winston to take an exam to enlist in the Army. Brian told Winston that he could receive money toward his daughter's education. That was good enough for Winston.

He went to downtown Long Beach and took the exam. The following day, Brian told me Winston had scored very high. A day or two later, Brian told me that although Winston did very well on his exam, he had two felonies on his record. My husband and I weren't aware of this. Winston didn't come around for a while after the military background check. I missed his cooking and conversation. We missed his unannounced visits and debates.

On April fifteenth, when returning home, I checked the messages on the voicemail. It was Winston's sister, Michelle. Tears began to stream down my cheeks. Winston had been shot and killed the night before by a security guard. His death had been covered on the local news. Many thoughts raced through my mind. Was Winston under witness protection? He had shared stories about helping a prostitute try to turn her life around and about encouraging other users to do the right thing. Many mornings after Winston's death, I waited for that early morning knock on my door, hoping that it would be Winston, ready to cook my breakfast and explain how he was able to fake his death in some elaborate undercover scheme. However, it never happened. Winston was gone forever—and not with a needle left in his arm, slumped over in some dirty gas station bathroom, but by bullets, three of them. Crystal is God. She reigns on Beach and Ball. Crystal is queen of the underworld. Crystal is Aphrodite, Lilith, Oshun, Erzulie, and Bastet, cloaked in a hooded black robe. She promised sweet sex and eternal orgasms, but delivered only death.

Rest in peace, Winston. April 14, 2009.

Death is Tailgating

(for Winston)

I have watched Death tailgate my friend.
His sharp turns, sudden taps on the brakes,
and Grand Prix skills could not out maneuver
Death's fixation on his fate.
Crystal Methology is my friend's
psychology,
and she's in the passenger
seat, with the window down,
smiling, wanting to paint
the whole town red before he's dead.
My friend's hands are gripped on the
steering wheel, tight and zombie like.
The smell of death
flows through tailpipes, and flashing reds
of motel signs and streetlights
control his nights.
As air blows through Crystal's hair,
highway patrolmen pass and stare.
His skeletal reflection
in their mirrored shades
is a detection that Death is near.
I am just a jaywalker,
rushing to avoid a deadly collision

as days and nights of bad decisions
pop his veins.
No bull's eye on my breasts
or daggers through my chest.
I may flirt with the mysteries
of the night, but I do not, will not flirt with
Death.

(written for Winston in February 2009)

Las Uvas Verdes/Las Manos Negras

There were Texans and Oklahomans
in those fields,
Texans and Oklahomans who made whistles from vines
and clapped their Black hands like they
channeled the Holy Ghost
on a Baptist church floorboard.
These workers charmed
bees and gopher snakes,
blew their souls through
metal harmonicas
while they swatted, sweated,
and whistled toward a brighter future
When they picked las uvas verdes with
their feet planted firmly on fertile California soil.
They left Southern impressions of
soleless shoes.
Las familias negras tackled rows and rows
of green grapes, orchards, and white afro puffs.
They hummed as if baked bread pudding or fresh yeast bread
waited for their palates at home on dining tables.

Heirloom Seeds

Mother Nature has tried.
She has tried to convince
us to spit her seeds
back into the cycle of life.
She has relentlessly enticed us to spit the
seeds into the cycle,
like the rotary part of a washing machine
But we have thrown a rusty wrench
into natural order.
We have created hybrid
crops that began in sterile white labs
and are spliced under
microscopes and sold in bulk
to farmers.
We have created
crops with motives,
jerking around our DNA,
zapping insects,
and mocking nature.
We are gods in white garb,
wearing thick goggles,
dispersing airborne—
not heirloom—seeds

into the atmosphere.
We are shameless and focused,
creating corrupted
files of produce.

Kings River Blues

2006

Selma, Hanford, and the whole San Joaquin Valley can get blistering hot. My paternal grandfather's journey moved from the laborious hot summers spent in one-room houses and wooden floorboards in Tenaha, Texas, to the city presently known as the raisin capitol, Selma. He has finally relaxed. His face displayed lines of hard work and wisdom as he sat in his tattered black recliner. He and the recliner were surrounded by hundreds of picture frames, antique boxes, knick-knacks, and stacks of photo albums. Sunlight struggled to break through the thick blinds and sliding glass door that shield his dank living room. He stands six feet tall. The frame of his body is slightly angled from aging, yet he still drives and is active. He's as competent and witty as ever. He told me about a female mule named Della and then made a clicking sound with his mouth like a South African warrior, demonstrating the command sound for Della. With the help of other male relatives, he built a wooden house in Allensworth, California's first black settlement. One year, my grandfather's story was covered in one of Fresno's local paper—the Daily Collegian. He had explained how he threatened a Caucasian man with an ax and a gun when the man attempted to take away his hard-earned clothes stamps when he lived in Tenaha, Texas.

My grandfather shared other fascinating stories as I sat propped in front of him with a voice recorder. Who is this man that I write of? He is my last living grandparent. This is the first time in my life that I have spent quality time with or even visited my grandfather. Friday, I spent the whole day with my paternal grandfather, who was born on February 12,1920.

It was such a rewarding day. I'm lucky to have a grandparent still with me. However, I don't know him. I know of him, but I don't really know my grandfather. I didn't meet him until my late twenties. So now I'm trying to play catch-up, which is rewarding, yet melancholic. I'm not sure if anything can replace those lost years, because I still feel disconnected, worlds apart. I feel as though I have "Kings River Blues."

I have fond memories of my mother's father, and I could say that I got to know him a bit more because of my mother. I remember my grandfather's tone of voice, his speech patterns, his smile, his laugh, and the way he tilted his head when I rode in the car with him. I have memories of him wearing a white undershirt as he fed hogs. I have no recollection of my mother's grandfather or my mother's mother. The only memories I have of my maternal grandmother and great-grandfather are passed down through my aunts and uncles who shared their stories with me.

I plan to visit my grandfather as often as I can. I wish I lived closer. I would go see him daily. But I'm thankful that he's still around. Every moment I'm with him, I'm mentally recording his behavior. I pay attention to the programs he watches on television, the jokes he makes, his diet—everything. He catches me staring at him in awe sometimes. How people can be involved in elder abuse or take advantage of the elderly is beyond me. People who commit such horrible acts should be burned at the stake!

My husband and I spent half a day with my grandfather Bumblebee and his wife Barbara, who is nicknamed Honeybee. And for the record, they gave each other these names.

Barbara offered to fry us some fish and chips, but first, she needed a few items from the grocery before she prepared our lunch. So we offered to go get what she needed. As we walked to the car, Barbara shouted out the door, "Bumblebee, show 'em the new buildings downtown!"

So we drove through downtown Fresno before we headed to the local fish market to buy the catfish nuggets, white bread, and a bag of potatoes.

In the kitchen, the cooking oil crackled and popped like liquid fireworks as the catfish fried. The aromatic portions of catfish breaded in cornmeal permeated the entire house. When Barbara was finished with the frying, we ate at the kitchen table and drank ice cold red-fruit punch soda. I gave my grandfather a birthday card for his birthday. My husband had recorded some blues music on a cassette for my grandfather, too. Interestingly enough, I share my maternal great-grandfather's birthday of February 9.

After lunch, I inspected my grandfather's patio, and from the number of fishing rods he had, he appeared to be an avid fisherman.

Kings River Blues Part Two

(for grandpa Buford)

Forgive me for staring,
but I ain't got no manners.
I can see the outline of
wings starting to pierce through the skin on
your back.
They're sprouting as you sit daily in your
recliner, watching television, and
your black leather jacket will not contain
them.
Your wings are fresh and young, like the
meat of green coconuts.
They're crackling, itching, locking, and
fusing to your spine right before my eyes.
They're growing and developing strong,
so I have no reservations
and am ruthless in my pursuit
for your information
knowledge
and
wisdom.
I will break bottles on bar tables
like contraband
and use the jagged edge to swing

and draw blood from negativity.
I am whiskey fierce,
narrow-minded, and focused.
I can hear the stomping in the Friendship
Baptist Church
on a little street in Selma,
the city where you finally settled in
California.
I can hear the claps of the sanctified
as they turn their head to the side,
and the ancient history of language is
jumbled and funneled
through their tongue,
sputtering off their lips,
trance enhanced,
rhythmic like drumming in Gabon.
Your journey has ended, yet war still
continues in this world.
Men are still fighting while holding their
holy books,
shedding blood.
But you, you made it! Hallelujah!
Babies are still being dropped in your lap,
generation after generation,
and you are able to hold them for a
few minutes just to hear them coo to your

harmonica playing the Kings River Blues.
Share with me what that feels like,
because tomorrow is not promised,
and no amount of money can buy
experience.
I can see the wings
breaking through the skin on your
back, and your black leather jacket
cannot contain them.

(2013)

Aromatherapy

I grew up on the scent of popcorn,
especially on Saturday mornings.
The aroma from the popcorn
factory on the corner of my street
drifted east with wind and greeted
many urban sunrises and storefront
churches.
It passed my front yard,
infusing my neighborhood
with popped kernels
and cheese flavor.
Distinct childhood tastes
like the popcorn,
tart lemonade berries,
and wine grapes
still linger on my palate.
My mother and father
grew up on the sweet smell of
hay,
truckloads of garlic and onions, and
the pungent odor of dairy cows.
I remember all these scents
collectively
because of my constant travel

back and forth on the 99 Freeway
for funerals or holidays
or kisses on the cheek from
lips masked with
thick layers of red lipstick.
I lived a farm life vicariously
through my relatives,
running through corn fields
or taunting bulls with my cousins.
I remember you, Hanford.
I remember.

The Grocer

I remember as a child growing up in Los Angeles in the mid-70s and being sent to the corner store by either my mom or neighbors. It was a yellow-orange storefront owned by a Korean couple named Tom and Sue. I remember being barely able to look over the counter and staring at a large jar of pickled pig's feet next to the cash register. As a child, I always thought a lot of feetless pigs were wallowing in mud on a farm somewhere near my grandfather's property. Tom's had its own butchers and sold milk and eggs, too. However, traditionally, stores such as this one sold only dry goods, while milk was sold by the dairy and meat by a butcher.

Recently, I visited a grocery store in Hanford that still offered grocery and household goods on credit to its customers. This grocery story had been in business at that same location since 1945. It's also nestled in the center of a community, where just behind the store, homes with front yards are surrounded by wooden fences and fruit trees.

Inside, the grocery store's counter was reflective of its owner, like a personal desk or bedroom. The items revealed a little glance into the character of the counter's owner. There were shelves of vintage family photos, rosaries, sketches of Native Americans, and various items from the owner's home. I could tell that Hanford, even in the twenty-first century had maintained its small-town charm and uniqueness. Located in the agriculturally dominated Central California, the financial habits of an independent grocery store in a small town can serve as the barometer for trust in a community.

Traditionally, grocery stores offered credit until a family's harvest could be sold. When people were hungry, they didn't have to put off buying food because they lacked the money. For sixty-eight years, this business survived among the Wal-Marts and uber supermarkets that sprang up around it. But convenience will never expire. If a person can walk to the local grocery store without getting into the car and spending money on gas—especially with today's gas prices—then they've already saved money before even entering the store, not to mention the hassle of searching for parking and standing in a longer line.

How About a Cup of Cow-Chip Tea?

During one of my many interviews with my grandfather and great uncle, the two brought up one seemingly disgusting cure for pneumonia and other common ailments in which they partook while growing up in Southern Texas in the late 1920s and 1930s. While most of us can't even fathom the human consumption of cow excrement, it was widely practiced back in the day.

"Oh yeah, it made you feel real good," my Uncle Fred exclaimed. My grandfather also opined that, with a little added sugar, the seething-hot cup of cow-chip tea tasted great. They sipped on the hot brown liquid after the cow chips were wrapped in cheesecloth and placed in a cup of hot water.

Elders often know of various types of odd remedies, which are dismissed by today's standards and considered to be "backwoods" practices. However, not all of these practices should be ruled out. Many of these remedies contain morsels of validity, even with the infamous, cow-chip tea. My family drank cow-chip tea that was administered by my paternal great-great-grandmother, Mary Ann Boulden Scott, who was a medicine woman and midwife. She delivered many, if not all, of her grandchildren at home, including my great-uncle and grandfather.

This practice of drinking cow manure was most likely influenced by Native Americans. In fact, it said to be among the many ingredients present in the peace pipe. Consuming cow dung and cow urine is also widely practiced in many cultural and religious sects of India. I found in most African countries, though, cow dung was mainly utilized as a biofuel and used for agricultural and household purposes.

Interestingly enough, cow dung contains the bacteria mycobacterium vaccae, which activates a group of neurons in the brain that produce the hormone serotonin. Serotonin is responsible for feelings of well-being and happiness. So it is no wonder that my great-uncle Fred said it made him feel good. According to my great-uncle, my great-great-grandmother used to send him out into the woods to gather up certain roots, bark, and herbs to make elixirs. She would hold up the plants of what she needed, so my uncle could get a visual of what he was looking for before he went out into the woods to collect them.

Even today, my great-uncle still practices the healthy beneficial knowledge that was passed on from his grandmother. He shared that the medical staff from the local hospital used to send patients to her because she was a licensed practitioner of alternative medicine. My great-uncle's front porch is lined with ceramic pots of aloe vera plants, cilantro, and various herbs. His refrigerator is filled with ginger roots, coconut water, and Greek yogurt, and his cabinets are stocked with cinnamon, garlic, curry, and pepper.

Does this mean I should go out and gather up dried cow dung and brew a fresh cup of cow-chip tea to have with my shortbread biscuits when I start my day? Absolutely not. Besides, cows these days are pumped with hormones, our top soil is horribly depleted, and what some farmers feed cows these days is reprehensible. Once again, we must share the knowledge and oral history that our elders divulge. This piece is a salute to my great-great-grandmother, Mary Ann Boulden Scott, whose wise-woman knowledge saved many lives during her time. In addition to sharing the knowledge, we must also research and read from a variety of resources based on what our elders reveal so that we can fully understand what's given to us and use it in a productive and selfless manner.

My Reflection about Picking Grapes in the 1950s

From my mother, Lorraine:

I started working in the grape fields at the age of twelve. My Aunt Betty was our guardian angel in the fields. Although Aunt Betty was only four-foot-eleven and we, her nieces, were much taller, she got our respect. We would freeze our drinking water in a thick large jar wrapped with burlap to keep the water cold as long as possible. We had to get up around three a.m. in the morning and had to dress as though we lived in Alaska. Mornings were always cold, dark, and sometimes foggy. We would have to put on two layers of clothing to keep warm. Our lunch consisted of bologna and cheese or peanut butter sandwiches. We also had to bring a knife to cut grapes off the vines. We stood on the corner close to where we lived and waited for this large truck, which always looked like it was about to fall apart. The drivers scared us to death as they turned sharp corners and sped to get to the fields so they wouldn't be late. If they were late, they jeopardized their pay. Every now and then, I thought the drivers were half-drunk. One time, we had just crossed a railroad, and the train passed by within in a few seconds. The truck had wooden seats on both sides and in the middle. If we were lucky to get picked up first, we would get a seat. Otherwise, we were hauled in the middle like cattle and sat on the floor. The truck had no closures in the back. However, sometimes, there would be two large canvases attached to prevent the cold air and wind from hitting us. The truck almost always carried men and winos who had made enough money to buy food and acquire liquor for their drinking problem. Most of the grape pickers were men. I only remember us in the fields, Aunt Betty, my sisters Judy and Connie, and myself. Before we arrived to the fields, the driver had to make about six stops to pick up other laborers. Once he'd finished with picking up the rest of the workers, it was about a two-hour or more drive to the fields.

Once we arrived at the fields, the owner would count how many grape pickers were present and then give the rules, the time we started, and the time we would quit. We worked from daylight at about six a.m. to around four p.m. Occasionally, they would provide us with large tin bowl-like containers to put the grapes in, and sometimes, we had to purchase the containers ourselves. During those early morning hours, it was so cold that we would build a fire to thaw out our hands before we started cutting grapes. By noon, the sun would beat down on us, and we would start shedding our clothes. The heat would sometimes rise to over one hundred degrees. We basically worked on our knees to get under the vines to cut the grapes very carefully. Each bunch of grapes was laid and spread out on paper trays in order to let them dry and make raisins. The trays had to be a certain length apart and filled completely with bunches of grapes, which were mainly the Thompson seedless grapes. We had no toilets, and the famer seldom let us use his. As a result, we girls had to find a private area, which was difficult because we worked closely with so many men. This was potentially dangerous because of the snakes and wasp hives hidden under the vines. My older sister Judy was stung in both eyes by wasps and had to be rushed to the hospital by the famer. She never returned to the fields. After that incident, we always shook the vines to check for wasps before we cut the grapes.

We worked in the fields because most of the families had many children, and the town didn't hire the so-called minorities who lived across the tracks. So the fieldwork was available for us even though many of us were underage to be working. Most parents of large families didn't have great jobs. So during the summer or winter vacation from school, we helped our parents with extra money to buy our own school clothes and have spending money.

As far as our pay was concerned, each tray of grapes was worth six cents. We had to wait until the end of the week to get paid. If the farmer was nice, he would allow us take some grapes home. We traveled all around the San Joaquin Valley to pick grapes—Fresno, Pixley, Delano, Visalia, Lemoore, and Goshen, to name a few.

Lorraine left Hanford and moved to Los Angeles in 1959. Her work experience is extensive. She worked in the aerospace industry for five years and the medical and mental health fields for fifteen years. Lorraine also has experience in electronics, education, and secretarial work. She began working at Hughes-Raytheon in Administration in1989 and retired in 2006.

Cutting Grapes in the Early 1950s

From My Aunt Connie:

Raising a family of six children, most of them about 16 months apart in age, proved to be a hard job for Cornelius and Mary Frazier. Finding jobs and ways to support them got harder and harder each day. From the age of twelve to fourteen, myself and two of my siblings wanted to make money of our own without having to chop or pick cotton.

Unbeknownst to us, our favorite aunt, Betty, had always come up with ways to earn a little money for those extra things that our parents could not afford at that time. Aunt Betty always gave us nickels and dimes and bought us unexpected birthday and Christmas gifts. One day, she shared with us and some of the neighborhood kids how we could earn some money.

"Cut grapes," she said. We went to bed early the night before our first day of cutting grapes. We were excited about our new adventure. Aunt Betty was at the house about four thirty a.m. So, still filled with anxiety, we got dressed in our work clothes, prepared an elaborate lunch of bologna sandwiches, some chips, and cans of soda. My sisters and one of my brothers left the house with Aunt Betty to catch a ride in the back of an old truck with wooden benches for seats. It was really cold and dark. I wondered why in the world people would want to leave so early in the morning just to cut some grapes. When we arrived at the grape vineyard, it was still dark, but I caught a glimpse of the sun beginning to rise. Half an hour later, the driver had us all get off the truck and assigned us a row of grapes where we were to start. Now my idea of cutting grapes was going into my grandfather's backyard and cutting a few bunches of grapes off the vines.

The Lord knows that I was not prepared for what I casted my eyes upon. Those rows of grapes seemed to go for miles… there was no end. And then we were given a large metal pan, an oblong wooden frame, and some paper that looked like the paper you get from a packaging company to wrap items for your boxes. The tool we used was a paring knife, like the knives we used to cut fruit. And to add to working within these lengthy rows of grapes, the weather was going to be a minimum of one hundred degrees.

"Okay, you brats, let's get started," said Aunt Betty. She would go about a hundred yards in front of us. When we got to where she'd started, we could move forward in front of her. When she caught up with us, she would go in front of us, and so forth. Cutting these grapes required us to be on our knees for the majority of the time. We were used to just reaching up about shoulder high and cutting off a couple of bunches. I wondered what we'd gotten ourselves into. After about an hour or so, Aunt Betty realized that we were stalling and waiting for her to get a long distance ahead of us. She was the sweetest aunt, and she knew what we were doing. But Aunt Betty was also determined to make sure we made some money.

About eight or nine a.m., the intensity of the sun's heat was extreme. As a result of the hot weather, we said we were tired and ready to eat our lunch. So Aunt Betty kept working while we ate lunch and played around. We then decided it was time for us to take a nap in the shade under the high grape vines. As we napped, all of a sudden, my sister jumped up, screamed, and ran down the row of grapes. After the sun heated up, the wasps awakened, and their home was, yes, among the grape vines.

Now, keep in mind, after the grapes were cut and put in the pan, we had to put the wooden frame on the paper down the middle of the row. Then we poured all the grapes in the frame and spread them evenly. By doing this, we allowed the sun to naturally dry the grapes to make raisins. Anyway, my running sister destroyed many of the grapes that were cut and spread out. Well, we finally got through our first day. Now, it was time to get paid. $1.50 was my first pay. Back in the early 50s, a dollar fifty was a lot of money for a youngster. In any event, I continued to work for the summer, making about two to three dollars a day. In addition, Aunt Betty always shared the entirety of her pay with us because that was her nature, and we all loved her dearly.

Connie worked for the Navy Exchange at NAS Lemoore, California, and the federal Defense Contract Administration Service Region in Los Angeles. She was a realtor for eight years and retired after eighteen years of service as an accounting technician for the Housing Authority of San Bernardino County in California. She has also received many awards for community service.

The Grape Experience

From my aunt Mary Sue:

Today in the grape fields of the San Joaquin Valley, the pickers are predominantly of Latino origin. However, from 1957 to 1961, I was a grape picker. I am a sixty-six-year-old African American woman who was born in Hanford, California, in Kings County.

My sisters and I used to cut and pick grapes every summer during school break. We had our fun times at the beginning of our summer vacation. However, once those Thompson grapes were ripe and ready to be picked, we hit those fields!

Our family lived on Second Street next to our grandparents, the Hardins. Every morning, Monday through Saturday, we had to be up at four in the morning to eat breakfast and catch the bus to the grape fields. Our aunt Betty and other adults always rode with us to the fields.

Some of the town's winos, men who drank wine excessively and daily, were among the passengers, Besides, they had to support their daily habit. I must admit though, I don't recall any of these winos causing any problems. Once we were in the fields, the grapes were nice and cool when we started cutting and spreading them on trays. However, once it was noon time, the temperature would rise to over a hundred degrees.

Aunt Betty was four feet eleven, and she would always take a whole row by herself. We younger siblings worked slowly and took many cold-water breaks. As a group, this slowed us down, but Aunt Betty would always come over to our rows to help us catch up to her. Saturday was usually our pay day. We only received six cents per tray. We didn't complain, though, because the money we made helped our parents purchase school clothes for the upcoming year. For me, those were the good ol' days, and it was the only work offered to African Americans during that time.

Mary Sue worked as a licensed vocational nurse from 1972 to 2004. She is now retired.

Picking Grapes

In my dad's own words:

During my younger years, the majority of the people picking cotton and grapes were Blacks and Whites. Three hundred trays of grapes were considered a good day, which amounted to about ten dollars. And picking four hundred pounds of cotton was good. My dad could pick between eight hundred and one thousand pounds of cotton per day, which was about twenty to thirty dollars. The Filipinos were in some type of group that Whites and Blacks could not penetrate or get into; they were paid higher wages in Delano, California. Cesar Chavez, at the time, was just a contractor, and I went to school with some of his kids. And we were all friends. The demographics of the fields did not start changing until about the 1970s and 80s. Also, we lived in Allensworth, California, for about two years. We all attended grade school in Allensworth with mostly all Black children. At the end of the school day, a trailer would pull up, and the kids that did not have a ride to the fields got in it and were driven to the fields where their parents were, in order to pick cotton until it was dark.

My father began picking grapes and cotton at the age of five. He and his siblings were accompanied by their father. He obtained an associate's degree from LA Trade Technical College, a Bachelor's of Science from the University of Redlands, and a master's degree from Pepperdine University in Malibu, California.

A Brief Note About Alex Horn, Jr.

Alex Horn Jr. was born in 1939 in Boley, Oklahoma, to Alsie and Alex Horn Sr. Horn arrived in Central California in 1949. Although Alex was not the only child born to Alsie and Alex Sr. I will focus on him because he is married to my Aunt Judy. She and Alex attended Hanford High School and were the first Blacks to be elected homecoming king and queen in 1958. During our interview, he recalled a man named Willie Brooks, who made a living from transporting Black Okies from Oklahoma and Arkansas to Central California in a huge truck, oftentimes covered with canvas. He charged somewhere between fifteen and twenty dollars for his service. Horn also picked grapes and other fruits during his youth. He went on to work for Lyles Construction Company in Visalia as a foreman. He also had his own construction crew. He is now retired.

Muddied water does not reflect. ~ French Proverb

"You have to know a river before you swim in it," my aunt Judy explained as she leaned over from her bed. She sparked my interest when she first spoke of the local rivers in the San Joaquin Valley. Kings River, the main river that runs throughout Hanford and the surrounding areas, was originally named Rio de los Santos Reyes. The name meant "River of the Holy Kings" and was given by a Spanish explorer to honor the biblical magi.

My aunt spoke of water as if it were a breathing, intelligent entity. "You cannot step in the same river twice," proclaimed Heraclitus. Rivers are fluid, feminine; they are yin. Rivers can entice the unsuspected visitor with a serene surface of soft ripples and yet have violent undercurrents that are hungry for life, hungry for blood. Rivers thrive with life in the form of animals, plants, and microorganisms.

“I will not get in a boat with someone who does not know how to swim,” she stated firmly. She didn’t want to take responsibility for adults who didn’t know how to swim because the likelihood of injuring or drowning yourself in the attempt to save another life is a reality unless you’re trained to do so. These principles of hers stem from a long-term relationship with bodies of water, especially with rivers. It’s important to know how to swim, especially since recent studies reveal that Black children are five times more likely to drown than children from other racial groups are.

Knowing a river is like knowing someone’s personality. Once you’re knowledgeable of a person’s attributes and flaws, you can deal with that person accordingly. The same holds true with rivers, and in this case, the Kings River.

My aunt was the first Black student at Hanford High School to teach swimming. She was born in Hanford on June 15, 1940, and currently resides with Alex Horn Jr.

Etheoiphia Palm Garden

"He built the first zoo in Hanford, and he built it alone," said Charles Blakeney, a distinguished educator based in Berkeley, California, during a phone interview I conducted in 1993. Yes, I started doing an in depth genealogical investigation on my great-grandfather as far back as 1993. Blakeney used many adjectives and phrases to describe my great-grandfather, William Joseph Hardin. He referred to my great-grandfather as "eccentric, mysterious, a visionary, and a pioneer." He was born in Atlanta, Georgia, on February 9, 1874. So perhaps this might explain my deep interest and admiration for him. It's as if I was meant to be reminded of his life every time I turn a year older—I don't believe in coincidences.

I remember learning about my great-grandfather's passing on February 14, 1973. Blakeney also described my great-grandfather as being "secretive" and "serious." And many things were revealed after his death. The first time my great-grandfather smiled at Blakeney made his day. As we wrapped up our phone interview regarding my great-grandfather, Blakeney stated, "I was inspired by the best."

For the record, my family members and I referred to my great-grandfather as "Papa," which is what I'll call him in the rest of this essay. In any event, the adjectives used by Blakeney also surfaced when I interviewed family members such as my mom, my aunts, and my uncles. Papa's paper trail was thin—disappointingly so. For example, I had access to his death certificate, but not his birth certificate. According to the Department of Vital Records in Georgia, a fire in the 1880s—if I remember correctly—had destroyed the record of Papa's birth. I had no idea what lay ahead of me as far as my research was concerned, but it has been a long, educational, and spiritual journey. Many of my elders believed that Papa came to California sometime in the early 1900s.

Etheiophia Palm Garden was the name of his zoo. This was documented in periodicals like the Fresno Bee and other oral accounts. Newspaper interviews with Papa mention that he worked briefly with carnivals and on railroads, but no other detailed information exists, that I know of. Various family members said that he acquired sickly animals from the carnivals and kept them on his property. I heard that Papa possessed everything from a Bengal Tiger to an ostrich. After several interviews with my family members, I surmise that Papa had a baby elephant, a crocodile, a lemur, exotic birds, and fish during the late 1940s and the early 1950s. I have an original admission ticket (see index). Unfortunately, my great-grandfather is not around to explain to us why he ran a zoo on his property or about the organization he started in 1911, called the Grand Order of Colored Christians, whose bylaws I discovered in one of his journals. There are entries in this journal dating back to as early as 1902. Almost on a daily basis, Papa used to wear a suit and tie and stand in front of a bank on Irwin St. and simply greet people walking by. He was an herbalist, entrepreneur, and pioneer and poet, and I think he was fascinating. He also ran a little general store where he sold food items such as candy, cheese, and bologna.

Papa also served in the United States military for fourteen years in Cuba, the Philippines, France, and Cambodia. He was also the grand marshal in the Kings County Homecoming Parade in May of 1971. He has one surviving son who resides in Southern California.

An Open Letter to My Dearly Departed Great Uncle, William Hardin Jr.

I wish I could have ridden the train to Mexico City with you to see the pyramids. What thoughts went through your mind as you made the several-hour trip? Did reflections of your future bounce off the passenger windows as you gazed at country landscapes and peasants? Did you consider staying and living among the Mexican people?

I can only imagine the adventures you experienced while you were there for two weeks. Uncle William, I have your gift of writing poetry. You slid handwritten poems folded in fourths to me when I visited you. I was in college then, and you were far away from where I lived. But in the few poems of yours that I have, courtesy of Aunt Judy, I can feel the passion in your writing. You were a true romantic. I interviewed Inez, your best friend of forty years. She shared with me how you sang to her in Spanish and Russian. She told me how you tutored one of her relatives in Spanish and how you helped Mexican immigrants obtain their documentation. Inez told me how you two prayed the Hail Mary in Spanish while you were close to your spiritual crossover.

Everyone, whether they were a friend, relative, or stranger, spoke of your fluency in several different languages—Armenian, Chinese, Russian, and Spanish, to name a few. The least I can do is include a couple of your poems in my book to pay homage to your talent for writing poetry and compassion for mankind. Thank you, Uncle William, for your guidance and inspiration.

My great-uncle William was a US Army Interpreter at the US Armed Forces Monterrey Institute of Foreign Languages. He was born on February 6, 1928, and died May 6, 1993.

Poems by William Joseph Hardin, Jr.

A Child's Prayer
(Lebanon)

I see no children in the square
since the first bomb fell that day.
They bombed the swings and happy things
and blew them all away.
Where I once played children's games
are foxholes all around and ugly tanks
and aircraft guns half-buried in the ground.
At night before I go to sleep,
I pray the war will end.
Dear God, please send the soldiers home,
and let me play again.

The Old House

It was just an old house with the walls painted brown
That stood on a hill on the outskirts of town,
The oldest house in the whole neighborhood
And the only house that was made out of wood.
The windows of the house had been cracked from the rain.
And large pieces of cardboard had replaced the panes.
The steps to the front door had half fallen down,
And from closed doors came every strange sound.
In front of the house stood a large Mulberry tree.
The long limbs seemed to hang from the trunk, oh so free.
A happier sight one could never see.
Then the tree full of berries all swinging around
And limbs of brown little bodies pulling them down.
No wonder the old house was so full of cheer
Whenever the ripe berries began to appear.

Now years have passed, and the old house is gone.
A large hole is there where the Mulberry stood,
And the little brown bodies have all made good.
They all live in motels and houses of brick and bright-colored walls,
oh so thick.
But every so often, they come into town and ask,
"What happened to the old house so free?
And what did they do to our Mulberry tree?"

The Photographs of Green Grapes Black Hands

Buford Joice in his early twenties

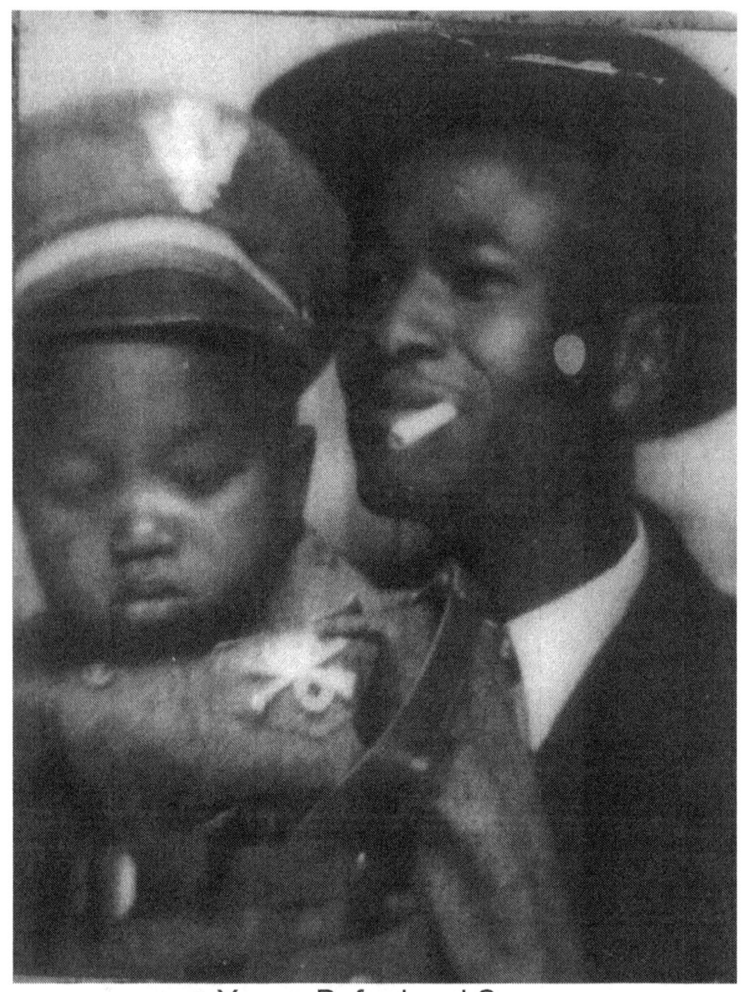

Young Buford and Son

Papa and little Jackie

Etheiophia Palm Garden Ticket

Papa's General Store

Photograph from early 1930's. From L to R William Hardin, Jr. my great uncle. Betty Hardin my great aunt Queen Mary Hardin my grandmother

THERE WILL BE AN

ILLUSTRATED ENTERTAINMENT

By **MR. WILLIAM J. HARDEN**, organizer and representative of the **Grand Order of the Colored Christians**, showing the progress of the Colored People's Christianity from 1713 to 1861 and the progress that we have made in the last 50 years by exercising the faith that we have in Christ Jesus, Our Lord.

THE SECOND NE BO

PROF. WM. J. HARDEN

Representative of the Grand Order of Colored Christians

Showing from whence we came through trials and tribulations; and to know that we know for ourselves that our Redeemer liveth; and that we are to day holding up the Banner and have declared within our souls that it shall never touch the ground.

The work of this Order is reserved. Come and see what the world is doing for us.

Admission

Flyer from William Hardin's Organization "Grand Order of Colored Christians

CALIFORNIA CONFERENCE
California District A. M. E. Church

[illegible]
5213 HOLMES AVENUE
J. N. WILSON,
[illegible]

Los Angeles, Cal. Nov. 9 1917

Mr. Wm. Hardin
Vallejo Cal.
My Dear Brother:

I am writing to say, first, at the Quarterly Conference held in Oakland Nov. 5th your name was proposed for license to exhort, and after due deliberations, was granted. I have no license blank with me; but on return to my office on or about Dec. 1 I will fill out and mail to you.

[illegible] to inquire of Condition

Spanish War Veteran Dies

[illegible] Hardin Sr., [illegible] of the Spanish American War, died this morning in the Veteran's Hospital in Fresno. Hardin celebrated his 99th birthday Feb. 9.

Hardin was a parade marshal for the 1971 Homecoming Parade. During an interview with the Sentinel at that time, Hardin said he "considered his life as having been a good one."

Born in Georgia in 1874, the veteran lived in Hanford most of his life between tours of duty with the Army. During the Spanish American conflict around the turn of the century, Hardin served the 48th Volunteers and 9th Cavalry in Cuba and the Philippines.

Following the conflict, Hardin was a member of an expeditionary force that surveyed parts of what is today Vietnam.

Hardin was in France with the 92nd Division during the first World War. During his long career, Hardin worked with carnivals and the railroad. He also worked for the border patrol for a short time.

For years Hardin operated a general store and cafe on front portion of his property at 115 W. Second Street in Hanford.

WILLIAM HARDIN SR.

Survivors include his daughters, Mrs. Josephine Brice, Los Angeles, and Betty Hardin of Hanford; two sons, William J. Hardin Jr., Hanford and Robert Richard Hardin, Sun Valley; a sister, Mrs. Viola Summers of Michigan; nine grandchildren; 15 great-grandchildren and several nieces and nephews.

Funeral services will be held at 2 p.m. Tuesday in the Odell Colonial Chapel. Burial will be in Hanford Cemetery.

Hanford Sentinel February 14, 1973

Cornelius Frazier, Sr. Heavy Weight Boxing
Champion in Tulare, CA 1950's Born in Denton,
Texas
September 26, 1917-Departed December 28, 1987.

Josephine Hardin, one of the first African Americans to graduate from the United States Cadet Nurse Corps. She also became a registered nurse.

Form 300–A (Revised May 1944)
FEDERAL SECURITY AGENCY
U. S. PUBLIC HEALTH SERVICE
DIVISION OF NURSE EDUCATION

Budget Bureau
No. 68–R145.1.
Approval expires
8–31–45

School of Nursing Fresno County Genl Fresno State Calif.

SERIAL № 127878

UNITED STATES CADET NURSE CORPS
MEMBERSHIP CARD A

Name of Cadet:
Hardin Josephine D.
(Last) (First) (Middle initial)
Josephine D. Hardin
(Signature of cadet)

Cadet's home address:
115 West 2nd St.
(Number and street or R. F. D.)
Hanford ~~Fresno~~ Kings Calif.
(City) (County) (State)

Cadet's age on date of admission to Corps 19

Date of birth March 12, 1925

Dates of admission to school: (Fill in all that apply)
(1) Originally ~~Feb. 10, 1945~~
(2) By readmission 02-10-5
(3) By transfer from another school ~~Feb. 10, 1945~~ 02-5-19

Date of admission to Corps

Date of prospective beginning of Senior Cadet period ~~Aug. 10, 1947~~ 08-

Date of issuance of Form 300, Certificate of Membership 3-10-45

Eunice A. Roth, R.N.
(Signature of Director of School of Nursing)

Do not write below this line (this space is for central office use).

Termination by— *Date*

Graduation 2-11-48

Withdrawal (*a*) (*b*)

GPO 16—40095-1

04

The hands of my great aunt Louise shelling peas

Alex "Leon" Horn Jr. reflects on coming to Central California in 1949. He was born in Boley, OK October 1, 1939.

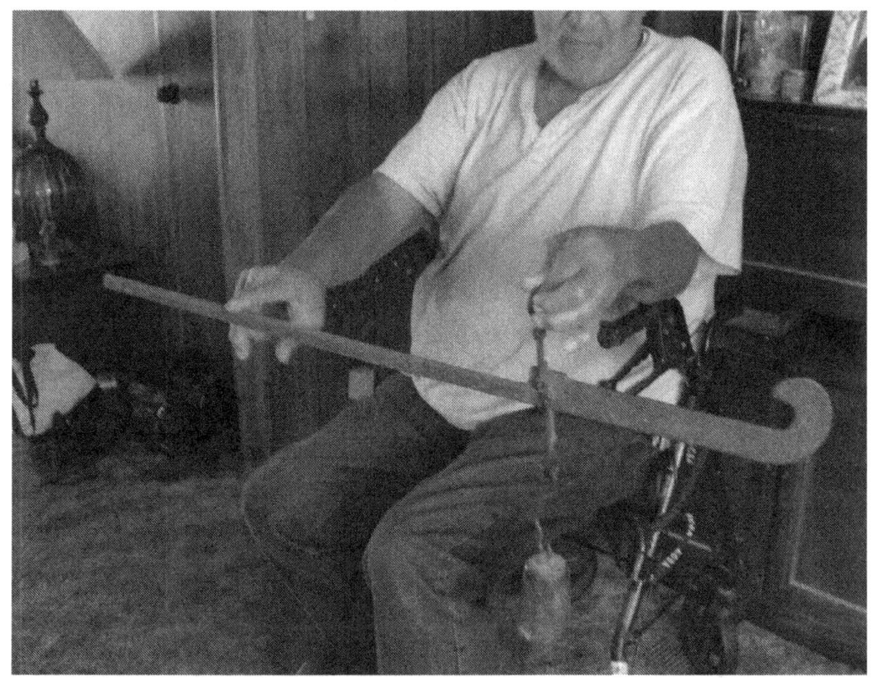

Here Leon holds up an antique cotton scale.

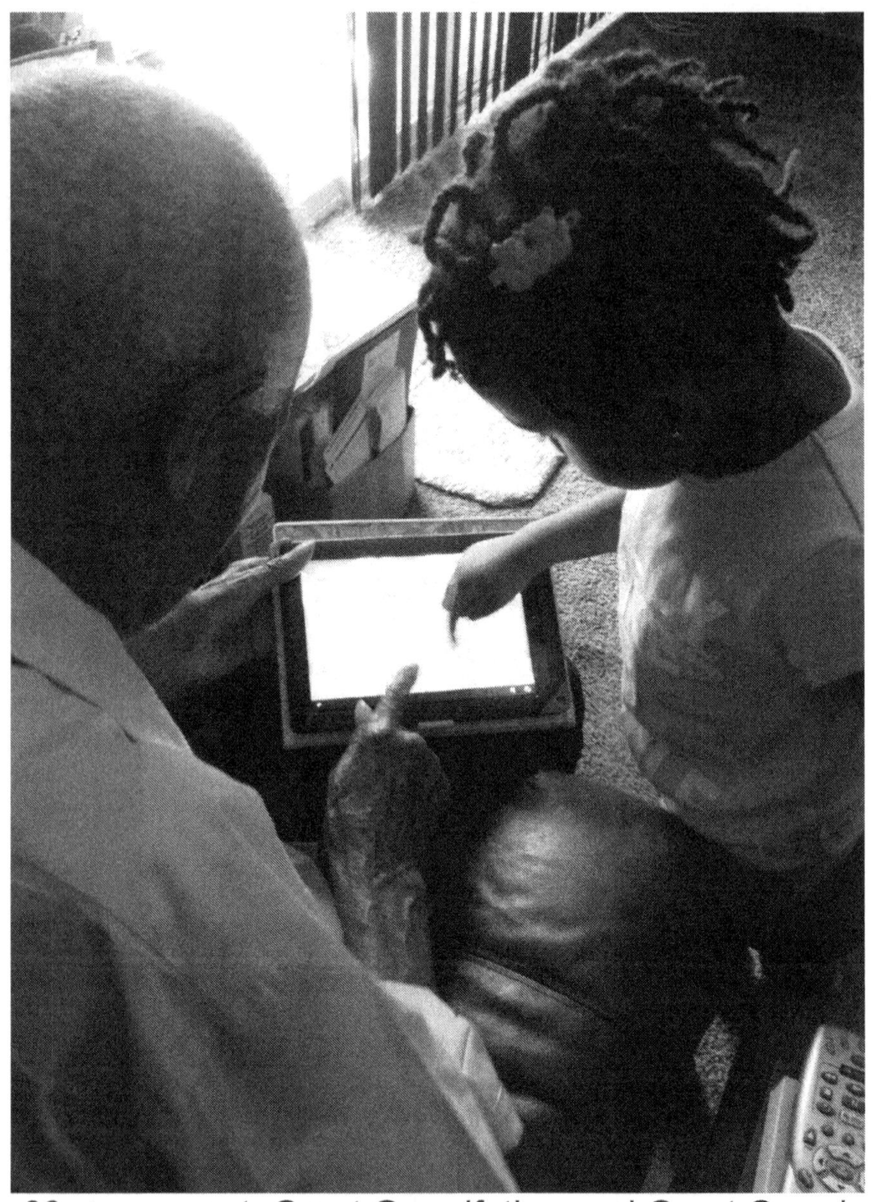

90 years apart. Great Grandfather and Great Grand daughter. Four generations... Buford Joice, my grandfather and Sunshine's great grandfather.

May 19, 2013, My grandfather Buford Joice

Letter from the Author

I'm elated by the information that continues to surface about the Black experience in the San Joaquin Valley. It is overwhelming, yet exciting. One of my goals for this book was to pique curiosity, inspire conversation, and perhaps encourage other descendants of the original African American families of the San Joaquin Valley to document and share the stories of their ancestors and relatives through film, song, rap video, or whatever moves them. I already know more books are to come on this topic, because I have been inundated with a wealth of information—more than a single book could contain. Documenting everything is important, especially in this digital age. I encourage individuals to print hard copies of important documents and articles and to keep them in a safe place. For example, on May 16, 2013, I attended a farmer's market in Hanford. Programs about the Kings County Homecoming Parade and events that upcoming weekend were being passed out. There was a section in the program that listed the past grand marshals, but my great-grandfather, William Hardin, was not listed. I contacted the chairman of the Kings County Homecoming committee and expressed my concern. Fortunately, I possessed a copy of the invitation extended to my great-grandfather to be the Grand Marshal in 1971, as well as the article in the Hanford Sentinel that mentioned it. I am thrilled to be able to share this journey of writing and research with the public and hope that this piece of work inspires other creations.

And So It Is

Jackie Joice

Afterword

Jackie Joice is an amazing storyteller and qualitative researcher. This book has changed my life while educating me about yet another contribution that African Americans have made to these United States. This time, in Central California in a town called Hanford. I had known about Hanford, CA, in Kings County, having visited my brother there for many years. I did not know however, about the rich lives of the Midwestern transplants in Hanford or the surrounding areas that made a life, and a way, for themselves. They had an incredible work ethic and love for family along with an unyielding desire to sustain themselves in this "new country". I am forever indebted to Jackie Joice for this very fine research. This is exceptional scholarship and it will probably be referenced for many years to come. Joice has done a fine job. This is, like the Warmth of Other Suns by Isabel Wilkerson a record of the tenacity and the shear commitment to life that these early African American migrants shared. Long before there were day laborers, and even long before Cesar Chavez organized workers for equality and humane treatment, there were Green Grapes and Black Hands.

I am deeply moved by the amount of time, attention, and love, which Joice has invested in this fine book. Joice is committed to uncovering every layer of love, work, power, relationship, motivation, and struggle of the "Okie's" and she does. Joice is committed to telling the truth while telling it with love and conviction. Joice is alert and provides the reader with a nuanced look into the lives of her family, the town of Hanford, CA, and the settlement by African Americans in the early twentieth century – this is an extraordinary ethnography that deserves to be lifted up, celebrated, and a model of dedicated family love.

I want to guarantee the reader that he or she will smile, laugh, cry, be stunned; that the reader will be a more educated, humane person after reading this fine book, and I do. Carefully read this book; take it all in. There is a lot to learn, to see, and to be lifted by... Joice is an expert storyteller.

Matais Pouncil, Ed. D.
Faculty
California State University, East Bay

Dedicated to the Black sharecroppers, migrant farm workers, and pioneers who traveled to Central California and paved the way for their descendants.

This is a partial list of surnames of the families who settled in the San Joaquin Valley:

Andrews
Blakeneys
Brooks
Crawford
Frazier
Hardin
Horn
Hurd
Joice
Jones
Joyce
Leathers
Morgan
Myers
Patterson
Ramsey

About Jackie Joice

Green Grapes Black Hands was inspired by her paternal grandfather's journey from Teneha, Texas to Selma, Ca in 1942. He bought his first harmonica in Texas for $.025. Her grandfather lived in the tent cities depicted in the classic movie "The Grapes of Wrath" directed by John Ford and based on the novel written by John Steinbeck. Her grandfather also lived in the first black settlement in California which was Allensworth. Joice's grandfather is still alive at the ripe age of 93. Green Grapes Black Hands is also inspired by her maternal great grandfather William Joseph Harden who arrived in California around the early 1900's. Harden started the first and only zoo in Hanford, CA. He also served 14 years in the U.S military. Harden was a Spanish American War veteran and was a member of the 1st US Volunteer Calvary known as the Rough Riders. He was recruited by Lieutenant Colonel Theodore Roosevelt and commanded by Colonel Leonard Wood. He was also apart of Roosevelt's 71st New York Regiment. He served in the 48th Volunteer and 9th Calvary in Cuba and Philippines (Buffalo Soldiers). Harden was in France with the 52nd Division during the first World War. Joice began her research on Harden in 1993. William Joseph Harden was born in Atlanta, Georgia on February 9, 1874 and died in Central California on February 14, 1973. This work emerged from the stories, songs, and sayings of her great grandparents, her grandparents, her parents, especially her mother, aunts and great aunts, uncles and great uncles. Lastly, Green Grapes Black Hands is Joice's wrath but also a glimpse into Joice's character and politics.

Jackie writes fiction , non-fiction and is also a spoken word poet and photographer. Her fiction and poetry incorporate her Catholic upbringing which has spawned into a hybridization of religious, witty and provocative writing. She has traveled to Cuba to study African-based religions in Habana and Santiago. She has also visited Ghana, West Africa and observed initiation rituals and interviewed practitioners of tradition based beliefs. In 2004, an excerpt of Joice's erotica novella "Fragaria" written under the moniker "Juniper Sanchez" was examined and discussed by her peers in the prestigious Hurston/Wright Writer's Week at Howard University in Washington, DC. Joice's photography reflects her style of writing. Her photographs taken in the city of Juarez were featured in the Badlands literary journal of California State University San Bernardino (Palm Desert Campus) in the Fall 2011 issue. Joice's essay and poem about her visit to Juarez was published in Shout Out: Women of Color Respond to Violence (Seal Press 2008). She has two researched entries in the The Women's Encyclopedia of Third Wave Feminism (Greenwood Press, 2005). Joice's novel Kanika's Burdens was published in 2012. Her poetry was recently included in the literary journal Song of The San Joaquin (2013) and The Lummox Journal (2012). Joice was a featured poet at Cal State San Bernardino's "Take Back The Night" event and UnSilence Autism (2013). She has several articles in Loudmouth Magazine (a feminist magazine) based at Cal State University Los Angeles.

About Glover Lane Press

Thank you so much for your purchase!

If you enjoyed reading Green Grapes Black Hands, please visit our website for our new, featured and upcoming publications.

www. gloverlanepress.webs.com
www.Facebook.com/Gloverlanepress

For an entire list of our print books and electronic books, you can also visit us on www.Amazon.com

www.ingramcontent.com/pod-product-compliance
Lightning Source LLC
LaVergne TN
LVHW012334100826
845148LV00017B/2365